THE CRAFT OF
COCKTAILS

THE CRAFT OF
COCKTAILS

Create the perfect cocktail

CONTENTS

CRAFTING FLAVOR

THE RISE OF THE CRAFT COCKTAIL

The craft cocktail movement really took off in the early twenty-first century, when there was an increasing preference for fresh ingredients, homemade mixers, and top-quality liquors. Cocktail bars across the world began to create more varied and interesting menus to cater for this growing trend. Artisan cocktails are now available in many bars and are defined by their use of natural produce and flavors, as well as by the more advanced mixology techniques it takes to make these drinks. These cocktails are more complex to put together than the basic classics, but the combination of natural flavors with premium liquors and liqueurs makes all the effort worthwhile.

Craft mixologists take fresh produce, such as fruits, vegetables, herbs, and spices, and either infuse these ingredients with alcohol to create exciting liquors with new flavors or blend these ingredients into the cocktail for a real hit of fresh flavor. On-trend ingredients that you will see in artisan cocktails include herbs, such as rosemary, basil, mint, cilantro, and thyme; fruits, such as berries, peach, plum, pomegranate, rhubarb, and watermelon; vegetables, such as beets, radish, carrot, cucumber, and fennel; and spices, such as horseradish, cinnamon, ginger, and chile. Other popular ingredients that are often used in craft cocktails include savory items, such as bacon or pickles; a variety of tea flavors, such as green tea or Earl Grey; and other more unusual ingredients, such as hot sauces, vinegars, and honey.

Artisan cocktails are also defined by the variety of new techniques that are used to make them. These techniques can range from making a basic foam for the top of a cocktail to using molecular mixology to create some truly eye-popping special effects, such as dry ice, or cocktails that change color. Infusion is also popular in craft mixology, from the simple act of adding some herbs to a liquor and sealing it in a jar to creating smoked liquors using wood chips. This book covers these techniques and shows how to create some exciting, modern craft cocktails in the comfort of your own home.

CLASSIC MIXOLOGY LIVES ON

Classic cocktails have an unwavering style that never seems to go out of fashion and traditional drinks, such as the Negroni or the Boulevardier, have recently enjoyed a resurgence in popularity again. The idea of the cocktail hour has a continuing chic and this book features some classic drinks from the golden era of cocktails, such as the Sidecar or the Tom Collins, that still possess an enduring glamour. So, as well as looking at the world of craft cocktails, this book contains all the classic drinks and mixology techniques to show how to create some timeless favorites. This book also takes some traditional drinks and gives them a contemporary twist, such as adding a vegetable infusion to a Bloody Mary to create a Beet Bloody Mary. This mixture of the classic and contemporary creates some stunning flavors and adds new dimensions to familiar favorites.

The chapters are broken down by technique: infusing and flaming; shaking and stirring; building and layering; muddling and blending; and using bitters and sours. These chapters guide you through how to master each of these mixology methods, and so you will soon feel confident enough to start creating your own craft cocktails and infusions, as well as mixing the amazing recipes contained in this book.

CRAFT TECHNIQUES

To create the perfect craft cocktail, there are a number of techniques that you will need to master. As well as the basic mixology techniques that are essential for any bartender to grasp, there are artisan techniques, such as infusion, seasoning, working with fire and ice, creating foams and airs, garnishing, and decoration. Essential techniques are covered within the chapters, so we look at infusing and flaming on pages 28–29, shaking and stirring on pages 56–57, building and layering on pages 92–93, muddling and blending on pages 122–123, and using bitters and sours on pages 156–157.

INFUSION

Infusion is everywhere in cocktail bars at the moment, from herb-, fruit-, and vegetable-soaked liquors to ones flavored with such diverse ingredients as bacon, tea, and wood chips. Infusions let you get really experimental and create your own unique flavors—this kind of freedom is rare in mixology, which usually involves using store-bought ingredients in exact amounts, so it's great for the more creative cocktail mixer.

In this book, there are a lot of infused recipes, using a range of ingredients, including rhubarb, peach, honey, ginger, green tea, beets, and rosemary, but it's worth taking time to test some infusions of your own. If you like a particular herb or spice, try placing it with a favorite liquor in a sealed, sterilized jar for a week. Taste and see what you think of the flavor; if you want it to be stronger, simply seal and let infuse for another week, or if it's too intense, add more liquor to dilute the flavor.

Another benefit of infusions is that you will always have prepared flavored liquors on hand instead of having to muddle the ingredients together each time. The depth of flavor should also be stronger with infusions, depending on how long they've been left to mix.

SEASONING

People don't often think of adding seasoning to cocktails, but using some subtle flavorings can add a lot to the taste and depth of your alcoholic creations. Traditional seasonings include salt and pepper for cocktails, such as the Bloody Mary, but modern mixologists are also using more complex flavors, such as herbs, spices, vinegars, chiles, hot sauces, horseradish, and even barbecue sauces, to enhance their mixes.

The most common seasoning is salt, which can be either dissolved into the drink or added as a garnish (see page 12 for how to rim a glass with salt). As with food, a lot of drinks can be improved with a pinch or two of salt, because it suppresses the bitterness of certain ingredients and enhances the flavors of others. Salt should be used sparingly, however, to avoid overwhelming the other ingredients. For Asian-themed drinks, a splash of soy sauce adds a salty, umami flavor and is especially good in smoky-flavored cocktails. Ground black pepper works well in Bloody Marys and other savory, rich cocktails.

Vinegars are used mainly in shrub cocktails (see pages 80–85) but can also be added to other drinks to create a tart, sharp flavor. The growing popularity of Kombucha-style drinks (fermented green or black teas) has added to the demand for vinegar flavors in cocktails and many bars now feature a variety of vinegar-seasoned beverages on their menus. Good types to use include balsamic, white or red wine, or sherry vinegars.

If you like spicy heat, you could experiment with using hot pepper sauce, chopped chiles, horseradish, or wasabi paste in your cocktails.

FIRE

If you want to create some real drama with your bartending skills, fire is the way to go. Flaming cocktails can make an attention-grabbing entrance when you serve these from the bar or kitchen and are good for parties or with a group of friends. When serving the on-fire drinks, always dim the lights for the full effect.

Creating a flaming drink is plenty of fun, but remember the safety basics. Prepare and light the drinks in an area that is away of other alcohol, cloths, or anything else that could catch on fire. Make sure that any glassware you use is heatproof. Do not drink the cocktail while it is still alight—cover the drink with a larger glass until the flames go out, wait for the flames to fully extinguish, and only drink the cocktail when the glass and contents are completely cooled. You can also blow out a flaming shot, but again remember to check that the flames have completely died down.

There are a few ways to light up a flaming cocktail, but the best way is to use a long match or a lit bamboo skewer; it will help you avoid potentially catching your fingers if the drink takes a while to catch. Hold the lit match or stick just above the surface of the drink until lit. Keep your fingers, face, and any clothing clear while the drink becomes aflame.

Stand back and enjoy the sight of the flickering flames—there's something beautiful about the effect of the fire reflecting off the glass and drink. Only let the fire burn for 5–10 seconds before extinguishing to avoid burning off too much alcohol and for safety.

There are some flaming cocktails on pages 50–53 for you to enjoy.

ICE

Adding the right kind of ice is incredibly important when it comes to mixology. The ice does two things: during the mixing process, it helps to chill and actively mixes the ingredients; then once the drink is served, it keeps the cocktail cold and prevents too much further dilution. Ice doesn't only chill; it also mellows the "burn" effect of stronger liquors and enhances their flavor. There are three main types of ice, each with distinctive properties that complement the drink, so be careful to use the right type of ice as instructed in the recipe.

WHOLE ICE CUBES

These are generally used to finish a drink, and the more ice you have in your glass, the colder your cocktail will be. Whole ice cubes can be made in the freezer with an ice cube tray—¾-inch cubes are the best size for most drinks. If you want crystal clear cubes, use filtered or mineral water or boiled and cooled tap water.

CRACKED ICE

This type of ice is generally smaller than whole ice cubes and is often used in a shaker to chill the liquid ingredients before you strain them. To make cracked ice from whole cubes, simply wrap the cubes in a clean, dry dish towel and give them a gentle knock with a rolling pin. The ice should be broken into pieces no smaller than half a cube.

CRUSHED ICE

This type of ice is perfect for blended drinks, because it speeds up the mixing process and freezes the whole concoction rapidly. Crushed ice is better for some beverages, because it means you can fill the entire glass with ice, whereas whole ice cubes leave greater gaps. To make crushed ice, wrap whole ice cubes in a clean, dry dish towel and knock with a rolling pin until crushed into small pieces.

GARNISHES AND DECORATION

The garnish or decoration is the final flourish that completes the perfect cocktail—both visually and in terms of flavor. Contemporary cocktails tend to contain a lot of garnishes and decorations, from bountiful sprigs of herbs to a splash of flower petals to add color and a fresh feel to the drink. Styling the look of the drink is an essential part of crafting a cocktail and an integral part of the bartender experience.

Garnishes can subtly influence the balance of flavors in a drink, particularly when it comes to lemon, orange, and lime peel, wedges, and twists. For peel or twists, use a vegetable peeler or knife to cut a lengthwise piece and try and keep pith to a minimum. Twist this piece just above the drink, rind side down, to release the citrus oil and hang over the rim or drop into the drink.

There are some basic guidelines for decorating cocktails, but most of it should be guided by your imagination and creative flair. One of the simplest rules is to match the decoration to the main flavors of the drink; for example, some sprigs of rosemary will work well in a Rosemary Vodka Cooler and make the cocktail look colorful and vibrant. Some pomegranate seeds sprinkled over a cranberry-base cocktail add both visual appeal and another fresh flavor.

Another way to add some style is to rim the glass with salt or sugar. You can use a specially made rimming dish, but a saucer is fine to use, too. To create a professional-looking rim, moisten the rim of the glass—either use some of the juice that is contained in the cocktail or use a sponge to apply some of the liquor from the drink. Turn the glass upside down and dip it into a saucer or rimming dish filled with sugar or salt—kosher sea salt and white or brown sugar all work well, or raw sugar forms attractive crystals on the rim of the glass.

FOAMS AND AIRS

Foams and airs are an alternative way of garnishing your cocktails and can be used to create a great visual effect—just think of the creamy, white head on top of a glass of dark stout for a classic example of a naturally occurring foam. Foams and airs can add an extra dimension to a drink and can be produced through a variety of techniques.

Foams and airs can be created in various thicknesses, from a light froth to a heavy, creamy foam. A simple way to produce a standard foam is to use egg white, lemon juice, and sugar; to top two cocktails, just whisk 1 egg white, 1 tablespoon of lemon juice, and 1 teaspoon of superfine sugar together until thoroughly mixed. This mixture can then be placed into a whip cream dispenser, charged, shaken, and sprayed over the top of the cocktails for a light, creamy finish. One thing to note is that the fresher the egg white, the more stable the foam, so try to use fresh eggs.

An air is an extremely light froth, with an effervescent texture that is less heavy than a foam—it can range from a bubble-bath foam to the fizz on the top of a glass of Champagne. To make a light air, the best ingredient to use is lecithin. Simply whisk a pinch of powdered lecithin with sugar syrup (see page 25), using a wire whisk or electric mixer, until a light air is created. If you prefer a finer air, use a milk frother.

TOOLS OF THE TRADE

GLASSES

Presentation is all in mixology, so it is important to serve a cocktail in the appropriate glass. The size, shape, and style all have an impact on the visual perception and enjoyment of the drink. Here are some of the classic glasses that you will need to have in your collection.

MARTINI GLASS

The most iconic of all cocktail glasses, the conical martini glass emerged with the art deco movement. The long stem is perfect for chilled drinks, because it keeps hands from inadvertently warming the cocktail.

HIGHBALL GLASS

Sometimes also known as a Collins glass, these glasses are perfect for serving drinks with a high proportion of mixer to liquor.

The highball glass is versatile enough to be a substitute for the similarly shaped, but slightly larger, Collins glass.

OLD-FASHIONED GLASS

The old-fashioned glass, also known as a rocks glass, is a short, squat glass and is great for serving any liquor on the rocks (over ice) or for short, mixed cocktails, such as the Old-Fashioned or Sazerac.

CHAMPAGNE FLUTE

The tall, thin tapered design of the flute reduces the Champagne's surface area and so helps to keep the fizz in the drink for longer. The flute has now largely replaced the coupe glass for serving Champagne and Champagne cocktails.

SHOT GLASS

This glass is a home-bar essential and can hold just enough liquor to be drunk in one mouthful. It has a firm bottom that can be satisfyingly slammed on top of a bar. The shot glass can also stand in for a measure when making cocktails.

COUPETTE GLASS

The coupette or margarita glass was previously the traditional way to serve Champagne, before the flute took over. Legend has it that the glass is modeled on a woman's breast. The coupette is now used to serve margaritas and daiquiris.

COUPE GLASS

Another glass with a wide rim that is good for serving sparkling drinks. The short-stemmed coupe is also used for serving daiquiris.

SNIFTER GLASS

The bowl-shape snifter glass invites the drinker to cradle the drink in their hands, warming the contents of the glass, so is good for winter liquors, such as brandy. The aroma of the drink is held in the glass, letting you breathe in the drink before sipping.

HURRICANE GLASS

This pear-shape glass pays homage to the hurricane lamp and was the glass used to create the New Orleans rum-base cocktail, Hurricane. It's also used for a variety of frozen and blended cocktails, such as the Piña Colada.

SLING GLASS

A variation on the highball glass, this is a design classic that is used to serve the Singapore Sling, the Long Island Ice Tea, and the Mojito. Its tall body and short stem make it ideal for chilled drinks.

MIXOLOGY KIT

What equipment you have in your home bar depends on whether you are the kind of person who likes all the latest gadgets or whether you are prepared to make do with the basics. Nowadays, there is no limit to the amount of bar equipment available, but you don't need a lot of gadgets to make most of the drinks in this book. Here are some of the essential tools of the trade that you'll need.

MEASURES AND JIGGERS

A jigger is a bartender's basic measuring tool for crafting the perfect blend of ingredients. Get a steel jigger with clear measurement markings, such as ½ ounce and 1 ounce, so you can easily and accurately measure.

BAR SPOON

A proper bar spoon has a small bowl and a long handle that allows you to muddle, mix, and stir with ease. Spoons come in a variety of lengths and widths, and a stylishly designed bar spoon is an attractive addition to any bartender's kit.

SHAKER

Most contemporary shakers are made from steel, because they don't tarnish easily and they don't conduct heat easily. This is useful with chilled cocktails, because the ice cools the cocktail instead of the shaker. Most standard shakers come with a built-in strainer, but if you have a Boston or Parisian shaker, you'll need a separate strainer.

MIXING GLASS OR BEAKER

Any vessel that holds about 2 cups of liquid can be used for mixing drinks. It is good to have a mixing glass with a spout or ridged rim so that you can stop ice from slipping into the glass, but this is not vital, because a strainer can be used. Mixing glasses are increasingly popular nowadays and are usually made of glass or crystal.

MUDDLER

For mashing up citrus fruit or crushing herbs, you need a muddler. This is a chunky wooden tool with a rounded end, and it can also be used to make cracked ice. You can do this job with a mortar and pestle but a muddler can be used directly in the mixing glass.

STRAINER

A bar or Hawthorne strainer is an essential tool to prevent ice and other ingredients from being poured into your glass. Some cocktails need to be double strained, so even if there is a strainer in your cocktail shaker, you'll still need a separate Hawthorne strainer in your bar collection.

JUICER

A traditional, ridged half-lemon shape on a saucer will work perfectly well for juicing small amounts. There is also a citrus spout that screws into a lemon or lime and is useful for obtaining tiny amounts of juice. Mechanical or electric presses are great for large amounts of juice but are not essential in a home bar.

OTHER EQUIPMENT

Other items you might need in your home-bar equipment are: corkscrew, bottle opener, fancy toothpicks, blender, tongs, ice bucket, cutting board, knives, pitchers, swizzle sticks, straws, and a whip cream dispenser for making foams.

PREMIUM INGREDIENTS

LIQUORS

Stocking your bar with top-quality liquors will mean that you can craft your cocktails with the finest blends of flavors. A good bartender understands the strengths and aromas of each liquor and knows how to combine them with a variety of ingredients to bring out their flavors to the full.

WHISKEY: BOURBON, RYE, SCOTCH, AND IRISH

Bourbon is a whiskey produced in the United States from a grain mash of not less than 51 percent corn. It is a sour mash whiskey, which means that the spent mash left over from the previous fermentation is added to each new batch. Tennessee whiskey, such as Jack Daniels, is similar to bourbon, but it is filtered through maple charcoal before it is aged.

Rye whiskey is mostly produced in North America and is made from a grain mash that is made up of at least 51 percent rye grain. Rye whiskey is not as sweet as bourbon and tends to be slightly peppery.

Scotch whisky has been made since at least the fifteenth century, and there are now more than 100 distilleries in Scotland, with a lot of small micro-distilleries springing up recently, too. There are two types of Scotch whisky: malt and grain.

Malt whisky is made only from malted barley and grain whisky is made from malt and unmalted barley, as well as other grains. Single malt whiskies tend to be more expensive, although blended whiskies can be of excellent quality.

Irish whiskey is similar to Scotch whisky, but does not have the smokiness of Scotch. Irish whiskey tends to contain malted barley plus a wider range of grains.

VODKA

Vodka has its roots in Russia, Eastern Europe, and Scandinavia. It is a clear liquor with a neutral taste, making it excellent for cocktails. Vodka can be distilled from any plant that is high in sugar, such as potatoes, sugar beet, or soybeans, although today vodka is normally made from a mash of grains, such as wheat, rye, or corn, and is filtered through charcoal. How the vodka is distilled and how many times it is distilled are important factors in its quality and flavor.

GIN

Gin is distilled from any grain, potato, or beet before being flavored with juniper and other herbs and then redistilled. Gin got a bad reputation in England in the eighteenth century, because it was so cheap that it was

more widely consumed than beer and was blamed for London's high death rate. Gin has seen a resurgence in recent years, with varieties such as sloe gin becoming more widely available.

RUM

Rum has a strong association with the Caribbean, where it was first made in the seventeenth century. Rum is made by fermenting and distilling molasses to produce a clear liquid that is often aged in oak barrels or colored with caramel to make dark rum. Rum can be turned into a liqueur and flavored with fruit or coconut.

SCHNAPPS

Schnapps is a catchall term for a liquor distilled from a grain or a fruit that is unsweetened. It is usually clear and has a neutral taste like vodka, so it is often flavored with fruits, such as peach.

TEQUILA AND MESCAL

Tequila and mescal are fermented and distilled from the agave plant that is grown throughout Mexico. Tequila is made from just the blue agave plant and only Mexico can legally produce this famous drink.

CACHAÇA

This is the national drink of Brazil and is an essential ingredient in the classic cocktail Caipirinha. This sugar cane liquor is the most popular distilled drink in Brazil.

ABSINTHE

Absinthe derives its name from the Latin for wormwood and is a liquor distilled from a mixture of bitter herbs, including wormwood, anise, angelica, and cloves.

PASTIS, SAMBUCA, AND OUZO

These are all anise-flavored liquors that are often consumed as shots but can be used in cocktails to add a licorice flavor.

SAKE

Sake is fermented rice wine that is clear and has a fairly neutral taste. There are many rituals involved with pouring and serving this drink in its native Japan.

LIQUEURS AND WINES

Adding subtleties of flavor to cocktails can be easily achieved with the huge array of liqueurs and wines available. Whether you prefer your cocktails sweet or bitter, dry or sour, or short or long, having a wide range of liqueurs in your home bar is vital for any good mixologist.

BRANDY AND COGNAC

Brandy and cognac are distilled wines that are processed and then aged in oak barrels for between two and ten years. Brandy was the first alcohol to be sold globally and is the key ingredient for many classic cocktails. Cognac is a regionally specific brandy that is distilled twice, in comparison to most other brandies or Armagnac, which are distilled just once. Brandy has a caramel color due to the aging process in wooden casks and is usually drunk as an after-dinner digestif; it is also a great base for many cocktails.

CHAMPAGNE

Champagne is the most famous wine-producing region in the world and is responsible for some of the most famous cocktails ever— the Champagne Sidecar and the Kir Royale, to name just two. Champagne is a drink that never seems to lose its style and, despite other contenders to the bubbly wine crown, such as prosecco, cava, and asti, Champagne is still the sparkle of choice.

VERMOUTH

A fortified wine with a vital place in cocktail history, whether shaken or stirred, vermouth is an essential ingredient of the Martini. Vermouth comes in three types: red, bianco (or white), and dry, which is the type used in Martinis. It is made with a complex mix of herbs and spices that varies, depending on the brand.

SHERRY

This Spanish fortified wine is made by combining brandy with wine and can range in flavor from dry to sweet dessert sherries. There are various types of sherry produced in different areas of Spain, such as pale cream, pale fino, light fino, Amontillado, Oloroso, and pale cortado.

PORT

Originally exported from Porto in Portugal, from where it gets its name, port is a red wine that is fortified with brandy. It is most often reserved for drinking as an after-dinner digestif and is often partnered with cheese. Vintage port tends to be unfiltered, so it needs to be decanted to remove the sediment.

AMARETTO

This is a golden brown Italian liqueur with a bittersweet almond taste. Its distinctive flavor comes from being made with burned sugar and up to 17 herbs and fruits.

TRIPLE SEC, GRAND MARNIER, CURAÇAO, AND COINTREAU

These are all orange-flavored liqueurs and are used in many cocktails to produce a sweet, citrus taste.

SOUTHERN COMFORT

A brand of American whiskey-base liqueur that is flavored with peach brandy, orange, vanilla, and cinnamon.

IRISH CREAM

A whiskey-base liqueur, its creamy flavor makes it a great base for more decadent, after-dinner cocktails.

MIXERS AND FLAVORINGS

As wonderful as alcohol is, you will also need to stock your home bar with a good range of mixers and flavorings to mix up a range of cocktails. The balance of alcohol to mixer is vital in achieving that unique flavor, so make sure you have all the essential mixers in your collection.

CLUB SODA

Club soda is similar to carbonated mineral water, but it has added salts, such as sodium bicarbonate. It is a neutral mixer that is useful for creating long cocktails without adding too much additional flavor.

TONIC WATER

A carbonated water that contains a small amount of quinine, tonic water gives cocktails a slightly bitter taste and is good with simple liquors, such as vodka and gin.

COLA

Cola has a complex mixture of flavors that brings a lot to a cocktail, with hints of lemon, orange, lime, cinnamon, lavender, coriander, and nutmeg. This allows for it to be used with simple ingredients to produce a still flavorful drink—for example, the classic Cuba Libre is just rum, cola, and lime. Cola works best with rum or whiskey, but is also good with neutral-tasting vodka.

GINGER BEER

Dating back to the eighteenth century, ginger beer is slightly bubbly and, in its naturally fermented state, mildly alcoholic. Its basic ingredients are ginger, lemon, sugar, and a fermenting ingredient, such as yeast. It is used in the famous cocktail Moscow Mule and combines well with vodka.

GINGER ALE

Ginger ale is a carbonated beverage that is similar to ginger beer but with a much subtler ginger flavor. It is also clear instead of cloudy, nonalcoholic, and has a dry flavor that works well in cocktails.

LEMON-FLAVORED SODA

This store-bought soda is a clear, carbonated beverage that is flavored with lemon. Along with other lightly flavored clear sodas, it is suitable for use in cocktails. Avoid using sodas with strong flavors, such as orange, which can be too overpowering for most drinks.

BITTER LEMON

Bitter lemon is tonic water flavored with lemon. The signature bitter taste is produced by the combination of the quinine and the lemon pith used to make this drink.

FRUIT JUICE

Store-bought or home-squeezed juices are both fine to use in cocktails, although home-produced juices will need to be

strained to remove any pulp. Orange juice goes well with vodka and tequila, pineapple juice is good with rum, and cranberry juice combines perfectly with vodka.

SUGAR SYRUP

This is a simple combination of sugar and water that is used to sweeten drinks. To make homemade sugar syrup, bring two parts of water to the boil in a saucepan. Remove from the heat and add one part of sugar, stirring to dissolve. (For example, you can use ½ cup of water to 4 tablespoons of sugar. Adjust the quantities for your needs, keeping the ratios the same.) Let cool, then pour into a bottle and refrigerate. This will keep for up to one month in the refrigerator.

ANGOSTURA BITTERS

Less of a mixer and more of a flavor enhancer, Angostura bitters is made from a blend of herbs and spices. It isn't in fact bitter when added to a drink, but is able to bring out the flavor of the other ingredients.

GRENADINE

Grenadine is a nonalcoholic, pomegranate-flavored syrup that is used to sweeten cocktails and to color them pink or red.

SPECIALTY SPICES

For some recipes in this book, you will need to buy some special herbs and spices. For example, to make your own homemade gin on page 42, you will need juniper berries, angelica root, orris root, and licorice root.

INFUSING & FLAMING

INFUSING & FLAMING

Infusions are a wonderful way to introduce some creative flair to your cocktail-making skills—you will be combining liquors and flavors to produce some inventive new ingredients that you can use again and again in your mixology. In this chapter, we use a variety of infusion techniques—from the simple method of combining liquors and ingredients in a jar for a period of time to creating fruit-infused syrups to add to your drinks. We also feature on-trend ingredients, such as matcha green tea and smoky bacon, to create some truly inventive, up-to-the-minute craft cocktails. For more on creating your own infusions, see page 8.

Flaming drinks are an eye-catching addition to any party or evening with friends, and, as well as looking impressive, igniting your drink can actually enhance the flavor. Lit drinks can be as simple as a flaming shooter or as dramatic as an on-fire punch bowl, but remember—when serving even the most basic flaming shot, dim the lights for the complete fiery effect. For flaming drinks, you'll need to use an ignition agent—in this chapter, we use 151 rum as the alcohol level is high, but any liquor that is at least 80 percent proof is fine to use. It is important to follow the amount specified in the recipes, because using too much flaming agent could be dangerous. For more on lighting your cocktails and for advice on fire safety, see page 10.

RHUBARB & VANILLA BOURBON COCKTAIL

SERVES 1

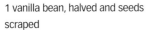

INGREDIENTS

1 vanilla bean, halved and seeds scraped

1⅔ cups fresh rhubarb, chopped

¼ cup sugar

1 ounce grenadine

1½ cups bourbon

½ ounce lemon juice

6 ounces pear juice

sliver of vanilla bean, to garnish

TIP

You could also try infusing the rhubarb with vodka, gin, or rum, but make sure you add the grenadine, because it adds a nice pink tone.

1.
This cocktail takes one week to infuse. Put the vanilla bean and seeds, rhubarb, and sugar into a saucepan over low heat and simmer for 5 minutes, or until softened. Stir.

2.
Let cool. Transfer the mixture to a sterilized, sealable jar and add the grenadine and bourbon. (Save the bourbon bottle for later use.) Mix and seal. Let stand in a cool place for a week.

3.
After a week, pour the bourbon mixture through a fine strainer, then strain through a coffee filter. Pour 1¾ ounces of the bourbon into a shaker (any remaining bourbon can be stored for up to two months). Add some ice cubes, the lemon juice, and pear juice and shake vigorously until well frosted. Fill a highball glass with ice cubes and strain the cocktail into the glass. Garnish with vanilla and serve immediately.

HONEY, PEACH & AGAVE INFUSION

SERVES 1

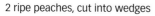

INGREDIENTS

2 ripe peaches, cut into wedges

10 peppercorns

2 star anise

½ vanilla bean, split

1 cinnamon stick

2 tablespoons agave syrup

2 tablespoons honey

1½ cups tequila

¾ ounce rum

¾ ounce lime juice

1 egg white

¾ ounce triple sec

peach slice, to garnish

TIP

For an alternative flavor, try using a combination of soft stone fruits, such as nectarines, plums, and apricots, instead of peaches.

1.
This cocktail takes one month to infuse. Put the peach wedges into a sterilized, sealable jar. Add the peppercorns, star anise, vanilla, cinnamon, agave, honey, and tequila. (Save the tequila bottle for later use.) Mix and seal. Let stand in a cool place for one month.

2.
After one month, strain the tequila through a fine strainer. Once strained, pour the tequila back into its bottle. Put ¾ ounce of the tequila into an ice cube-filled cocktail shaker. The rest of the tequila can be stored for up to two months. Add the rum, lime juice, egg white, and triple sec.

3.
Shake vigorously until well frosted. Strain into an ice cube-filled old-fashioned glass and garnish with the peach slice. Serve immediately.

Infusing & Flaming

PLUM & GINGER WHISKEY FIZZ

SERVES 1

INGREDIENTS

6 ripe plums, coarsely chopped

large piece of fresh ginger, peeled and sliced

2 tablespoons granulated sugar

3 whole cloves

1½ cups whiskey

¾ ounce lemon juice

6 ounces club soda

lemon slice, to garnish

TIP
This is the perfect drink for starting off a cocktail party and is guaranteed to create a party atmosphere.

1.
This cocktail takes one week to infuse. Put the plums, ginger, sugar, and cloves into a saucepan. Place over low heat and cook for 5 minutes. Let cool. Put the mixture into a sterilized, sealable jar. Add the whiskey and mix. (Save the whiskey bottle for later use.) Seal and let stand in a cool place for one week.

2.
After one week, pour the whiskey through a fine strainer, then strain through a coffee filter. Once strained, pour the whiskey back into its bottle. Put 1¾ ounces of the whiskey into an ice cube-filled cocktail shaker. The rest of the whiskey can be stored and used for up to two months. Add the lemon juice to the cocktail shaker. Shake vigorously until well frosted, then pour into an ice cube-filled highball glass. Top up with club soda and garnish with a lemon slice. Serve immediately.

PEACH & BASIL GIN FIX

SERVES 1

INGREDIENTS

1 ripe peach, cut into thin slices

4 ounces water

½ cup superfine sugar

12 basil leaves

1¾ ounces gin

¾ ounce lemon juice

peach slices and basil leaves,
to garnish (optional)

TIP

For a classic gin fix, omit the peach
and basil when making the syrup.

1.

Put the peach slices, water, and sugar
into a saucepan and bring to a boil
over high heat. Add the basil leaves,
then remove from the heat and let
cool. Once cooled, strain the liquid
through a fine strainer and store in a
sterilized, sealable jar.

2.

Fill an old-fashioned glass with
crushed ice. Add ¾ ounce of the
peach-infused syrup to the glass,
then add the gin and lemon juice.
Any remaining syrup should be
stored in the refrigerator and used
within one week.

3.

Stir well and garnish the glass with
the peach slices and basil leaves, if
using. Serve immediately.

MATCHA GREEN TEA VODKA REFRESHER

SERVES 1

INGREDIENTS

1½ cups vodka

1 teaspoon matcha green tea powder

2 small cinnamon sticks

1 teaspoon honey

1 teaspoon lemon juice

¾ ounce apple cider

1 small cinnamon stick, to garnish

TIP
This is a refreshing drink to start off a Friday evening after a long week at work.

1.
This cocktail takes 24 hours to infuse. Pour the vodka into a sterilized, sealable jar. (Save the vodka bottle for later use.) Add the green tea and the cinnamon sticks. Mix, then seal and let stand in a cool place for 24 hours.

2.
After 24 hours, remove the cinnamon and strain through a coffee filter. Pour the infused vodka back into its bottle.

3.
Chill a coupe glass. Put 1¾ ounces of the infused vodka into an ice cube-filled cocktail shaker. The rest of the vodka can be stored for up to two months. Add the honey, lemon, and apple cider.

4.
Shake vigorously until well frosted, then strain the cocktail into the glass. Garnish with the cinnamon stick and serve immediately.

BEET VIRGIN MARY

SERVES 1

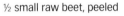

INGREDIENTS

½ small raw beet, peeled

6 ounces tomato juice

1 teaspoon Worcestershire sauce

¼ teaspoon celery salt

¼ teaspoon pepper

1 teaspoon freshly grated horseradish

½ teaspoon hot pepper sauce

1 lemon slice, to garnish

celery stalk, to garnish

TIP

If you're feeling adventurous, try swapping the tomato juice for Clamato juice and add your favorite fiery hot sauce.

1.
Cut the beet into small pieces. Put into a cocktail shaker and crush thoroughly with a muddler or pestle to release the color and flavor.

2.
Add the tomato juice, Worcestershire sauce, celery salt, pepper, horseradish, and hot pepper sauce. Stir well with a bar spoon.

3.
Pour the mixture into a Collins or highball glass.

4.
Add some ice cubes and stir again.

5.
Garnish the drink with the lemon slice and celery stalk. Serve immediately.

HOMEMADE GIN

MAKES 4¼ CUPS

INGREDIENTS

3 cups vodka

20 juniper berries

1¼ teaspoons dried cut angelica root

¾ teaspoon dried cut orris root

5 teaspoons coriander seeds

1 teaspoon dried cut licorice root

1 teaspoon orange peel

1 teaspoon lemon peel

TIP
For alternative flavors, you can also add other ingredients, such as cardamom pods, cassia bark, ginger root, rose petals, and nutmeg, to give it your own twist.

1.
This cocktail takes 48 hours to infuse. Put the vodka and all the ingredients, except the orange and lemon peel, into a sterilized, sealable jar. (Save the vodka bottle for later use.) Seal the jar and let infuse for 24 hours.

2.
Add the orange and lemon peel and let infuse for an additional 24 hours. The reason for adding the peels later is to keep the citrus notes fresh and to stop it from becoming too bitter.

3.
Strain the mixture through a strainer, then strain again through cheesecloth.

4.
Pour back into the vodka bottle and serve when needed.

ROSEMARY VODKA COOLER

SERVES 1

INGREDIENTS

1½ cups vodka

2 sprigs of rosemary

½ ounce sugar syrup

½ ounce lime juice

5 ounces ginger beer

rosemary sprigs and lime slices,
to garnish

TIP
For an extra ginger hit, replace the
rosemary with 1 cup of freshly
sliced ginger.

1.
This cocktail takes one week to infuse.
Put the vodka in a sterilized, sealable
bottle or jar and add the rosemary
sprigs. Seal and let infuse for
one week.

2.
Once infused, put 1¾ ounces of the
rosemary vodka into an ice cube-filled
Collins or highball glass.

3.
Add the sugar syrup and lime juice to
the glass. Top up with the ginger beer
and stir.

4.
Garnish with the rosemary and lime
slices. Serve immediately.

BACON & MAPLE COCKTAIL

SERVES 1

INGREDIENTS

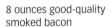

8 ounces good-quality smoked bacon

1½ cups bourbon

¾ ounce apple brandy

¾ ounce maple syrup

¾ ounce fresh lemon juice

1 egg white

¼ teaspoon apple pie spice

1.
This cocktail takes two to three days to infuse. Cook the bacon in a skillet over medium heat for 5 minutes, or until the fat has melted. Carefully strain the bacon fat through a fine strainer into a bowl and let cool slightly. Set aside the bacon.

2.
Pour the fat into a sterilized, sealable jar. Add the bourbon and seal. Shake vigorously for a few seconds, then put into a refrigerator for two or three days. Make a hole in the fat with a spoon. Strain the bourbon through cheesecloth back into its bottle. Place ice cubes into a cocktail shaker. Pour in ¾ ounce of the bourbon (the rest can be stored for up to two months), the apple brandy, maple syrup, lemon juice, and egg white. Shake until well frosted. Strain into an old-fashioned glass filled with ice cubes. Dust with the spice and serve immediately.

Infusing & Flaming

CIDER & RASPBERRY SLUSHIE

SERVES 1

INGREDIENTS

2 cups hard cider

1¼ cups fresh raspberries, plus 2 to garnish

TIP

For a nonalcoholic version of this, try using lemon-flavored soda instead of hard cider and experiment with different berries, such as blackberries, strawberries, or blueberries.

1.
Pour the hard cider into a freezer-proof plastic container with a lid.

2.
Secure the container with the lid and place in the freezer for 3 hours, or until the cider has frozen.

3.
Remove the cider from the freezer and break up the mixture with a fork, until the cider is in small chunks.

4.
Put the raspberries into a blender with the cider chunks and blend until you have a slushie consistency.

5.
Serve immediately in a large glass with a straw and garnish with the fresh raspberries.

HAZELNUT VODKA ESPRESSO

SERVES 1

INGREDIENTS

¾ ounce espresso

1¾ ounces Frangelico hazelnut liqueur

½ ounce vodka

½ teaspoon superfine sugar

1 marshmallow

½ ounce 151 rum

FACT

This is a great little treat for after dinner—just turn down the lights and serve flaming.

1.
Pour the espresso, Frangelico, vodka, and sugar into an ice cube-filled cocktail shaker.

2.
Shake vigorously until well frosted. Strain into a heatproof coupe or coupette glass.

3.
Place the marshmallow on top of the cocktail. Gently pour the 151 rum over the marshmallow.

4.
Set the marshmallow alight, using a long match, then let the flames die down completely and check the marshmallow and glass have cooled before drinking.

FLAMING CUCUMBER SAKE

SERVES 1

INGREDIENTS

1 small cucumber, thinly sliced lengthwise

1½ cups sake

10 peppercorns

1 long, thin cucumber slice

¾ ounce vodka

½ ounce lime juice

¾ ounce sugar syrup

½ ounce 151 rum

1.
This cocktail takes 24 hours to infuse. Put the cucumber, sake, and peppercorns in a sterilized, sealable jar. Seal and let stand in a cool place for 24 hours. (Save the sake bottle for later use.)

2.
Strain the sake through a fine strainer. Once strained, pour the sake back into its bottle.

3.
Place the cucumber slice around the inside of a heatproof old-fashioned glass, then add a few ice cubes. Pour ¾ ounce of the infused sake, the vodka, lime juice, and sugar syrup into a ice cube-filled cocktail shaker. The rest of the sake can be stored and used for up to two months.

4.
Shake vigorously until well frosted. Strain into the glass. Gently pour the 151 rum into the glass over the back of a teaspoon, so it sits on top of the drink. Set alight, using a long match, then let the flames die down and the drink cool completely before drinking.

FLAMING MAI TAI

SERVES 1

1.
Put the ice cubes into a cocktail shaker. Pour the rum, triple sec, brandy, pineapple juice, and almond syrup over the ice.

2.
Shake vigorously until well frosted. Fill a heatproof hurricane glass with ice cubes, then strain the cocktail into the glass.

3.
Place the chopped pineapple, cinnamon, and 151 rum into a mixing glass. Stir with a bar spoon to combine.

4.
Tilt the mixing glass and light the rum mixture with a long match. With care and using flame-resistant gloves, pour the lit rum mixture into the cocktail in the hurricane glass.

5.
Let the flames die down and the drink cool completely before drinking. Garnish with mint leaves and serve.

INGREDIENTS

¾ ounce brown rum

½ ounce triple sec

½ ounce brandy

4 ounces pineapple juice

½ ounce almond syrup

⅓ cup chopped fresh pineapple

½ teaspoon cinnamon

½ ounce 151 rum

mint leaves, to garnish

SHAKING & STIRRING

SHAKING & STIRRING

These are the two most basic mixology techniques, but they are essential to master to be able to confidently make a range of both classic and craft cocktails. Shaking is when you add all of the ingredients, with the specified amount of ice cubes, to the shaker and then shake vigorously for 5–10 seconds. The benefits of shaking are that the drink is rapidly mixed, chilled, and aerated. Once the drink has been shaken, the outside of the shaker should be lightly frosted.

Shaking a cocktail also dilutes the drink significantly. This dilution is an essential part of the cocktail-making process and gives shaken recipes the correct balance of taste, strength, and temperature. The drink is then double strained into glasses: the shaker should have a built-in strainer, but you usually use a separate strainer over the glass, too. Shaking can also be used to prepare cocktails that include an ingredient, such as an egg white, that will not combine well with less vigorous forms of mixing.

Stirring is the purist's choice. It's where you add all the ingredients, usually with some ice cubes, but this time you combine them in a mixing glass or beaker and then stir the ingredients together, using a long-handle bar spoon or swizzle stick. As with shaking, this lets you blend and chill the ingredients without too much erosion of the ice, so you can control the level of dilution and keep it to a minimum. This simple technique is important for drinks that do not need a lot of dilution, such as the classic Dry Martini.

TURKISH DELIGHT GIN COCKTAIL

SERVES 1

INGREDIENTS

1¾ ounces gin

6 ounces cranberry juice

1 tablespoon honey

¼ teaspoon rosewater

1 tablespoon pomegranate seeds

¼ teaspoon dried rose petals, plus extra to garnish

TIP
If you really love a floral taste, try using lavender petals instead of rose petals and lavender honey instead of normal honey.

1.
Pour the gin, cranberry juice, honey, and rosewater into a Collins or highball glass.

2.
Stir with a bar spoon until the honey has dissolved.

3.
Add a few ice cubes, pomegranate seeds, and rose petals, then stir again.

4.
Garnish with the rose petals and serve immediately with a straw.

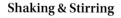

BOULEVARDIER

SERVES 1

1.
Place a handful of ice cubes into a cocktail shaker.

2.
Pour the bourbon, vermouth, and Campari over the ice, then stir well with a bar spoon.

3.
Strain the cocktail into a chilled coupe or coupette glass.

4.
Garnish with the lemon twist and serve immediately.

INGREDIENTS

1½ ounces bourbon

¾ ounce sweet vermouth

¾ ounce Campari

1 lemon twist, to garnish

MANHATTAN

SERVES 1

1.
Put cracked ice into a cocktail shaker.

2.
Pour the liquid ingredients over the cracked ice.

3.
Shake vigorously until well frosted.

4.
Strain into a chilled martini glass and garnish with the cherry. Serve immediately.

INGREDIENTS

1 teaspoon Angostura bitters

2½ ounces rye whiskey

¾ ounce sweet vermouth

cocktail cherry, to garnish

WHISKEY SLING

SERVES 1

INGREDIENTS

1 teaspoon confectioners' sugar

¾ ounce lemon juice

1 teaspoon water

1¾ ounces blended whiskey

orange wedge, to garnish

1.
Put the sugar into a mixing glass.

2.
Add the lemon juice and water and stir until the sugar has dissolved.

3.
Pour in the whiskey and stir to mix.

4.
Fill a small chilled old-fashioned glass halfway with cracked ice and strain the cocktail over it. Garnish with the orange wedge. Serve immediately.

MARGARITA

SERVES 1

INGREDIENTS

2 lime wedges

kosher salt

2½ ounces white tequila

¾ ounce triple sec

1¾ ounces lime juice

1.
Rub the rim of a chilled martini glass with a lime wedge.

2.
Dip the rim into a saucer of kosher salt.

3.
Put cracked ice into a cocktail shaker. Pour the tequila, triple sec, and lime juice over the ice and shake vigorously until well frosted. Strain into the glass.

4.
Garnish with the remaining lime wedge. Serve immediately.

Shaking & Stirring

GIN RICKEY

SERVES 1

1.
Fill a chilled highball glass or goblet with cracked ice.

2.
Pour the gin and lime juice over the ice. Top up with the club soda.

3.
Stir gently to mix and garnish with a lemon slice. Serve immediately.

INGREDIENTS

1¾ ounces gin

¾ ounce lime juice

club soda

lemon slice, to garnish

MARTINI

SERVES 1

1.
Put cracked ice into a cocktail shaker.

2.
Pour the gin and vermouth over the ice.

3.
Shake until well frosted. Strain into a chilled martini glass.

4.
Garnish with the olive. Serve immediately.

INGREDIENTS

2½ ounces gin

1 teaspoon dry vermouth, or to taste

cocktail olive, to garnish

RUM COBBLER

SERVES 1

INGREDIENTS

1 cup whiskey-barrel wood chips

1½ cups brown rum

splash of grenadine

½ ounce maraschino liqueur

maraschino cherry, orange slices, and
lime slices, to garnish

TIP

For a variation of this drink, substitute
¾ ounce of the rum for ¾ ounce of port
and add a splash of pineapple juice.

1.
This cocktail takes two weeks to infuse
and you will need a chef's torch. Lay
the whiskey-barrel chips on a metal
tray and place on a heatproof surface.

2.
Using a chef's torch, scorch the wood
chips all over until about half have
blackened. Put the scorched wood
chips into a sterilized, sealable jar, then
pour in the rum. (Save the rum bottle
for later use.) Mix and seal the jar. Let
stand in a cool place for two weeks.

3.
After two weeks, strain the rum
through a fine strainer. Fill an old-
fashioned glass with crushed ice. Pour
in 1¾ ounces of the rum. The rest can
be stored for up to two months.

4.
Add the grenadine and maraschino
and stir. Garnish with the cherry,
orange, and lime. Serve immediately.

GIN SWIZZLE

SERVES 1

INGREDIENTS

1 cup whiskey-barrel wood chips

1½ cups gin

¾ ounce lime juice

2 teaspoons superfine sugar

1 teaspoon Angostura bitters

6 ounces club soda

lime slice, to garnish

FACT

The swizzle originates from the West Indies, from sometime around the early 1900s. This version is made with whiskey-barrel smoked gin.

1.
This cocktail takes two weeks to infuse and you will need a chef's torch. Lay the wood chips on a metal tray and place onto a heatproof surface.

2.
Using a chef's torch, scorch the wood chips all over until about half have blackened. Put the scorched wood chips into a sterilized, sealable jar, then pour in the gin. (Save the gin bottle for later use.) Mix and seal the jar. Let stand in a cool place for two weeks.

3.
Strain the gin through a fine strainer. Put 1¾ ounces of smoked gin, the lime juice, superfine sugar, and bitters into a highball glass. The rest of the gin can be stored for up to two months. Add crushed ice to the glass and top up with the club soda. Froth well with a swizzle stick and serve immediately with a lime slice.

Shaking & Stirring

TOM COLLINS

SERVES 1

1.
Put cracked ice into a cocktail shaker.

2.
Pour the gin, lemon juice, and sugar syrup over the ice and shake vigorously until well frosted.

3.
Strain the cocktail into a chilled Collins or highball glass.

4.
Top up with club soda and garnish with the lemon slice. Serve immediately.

INGREDIENTS

2½ ounces gin

1¾ ounces lemon juice

½ ounce sugar syrup

club soda

lemon slice, to garnish

BLACK RUSSIAN

SERVES 1

1.
Pour the vodka and coffee liqueur over cracked ice into a chilled old-fashioned glass.

2.
Stir well with a bar spoon to mix.

3.
Serve immediately.

INGREDIENTS

1¾ ounces vodka

¾ ounce coffee liqueur

Shaking & Stirring

CUBA LIBRE

SERVES 1

1.
Fill a highball glass halfway with cracked ice.

2.
Pour the rum over the ice.

3.
Top up with cola.

4.
Stir gently to mix and garnish with the lime wedge. Serve immediately.

INGREDIENTS

1¾ ounces white rum

cola

lime wedge, to garnish

BVD

SERVES 1

1.
Pour the brandy, dry vermouth, and Dubonnet over cracked ice in a mixing glass.

2.
Stir to mix and strain into a chilled coupe glass. Serve immediately.

INGREDIENTS

¾ ounce brandy

¾ ounce dry vermouth

¾ ounce Dubonnet

GINGER WHISKY MAC

SERVES 1

1.
Pour the Scotch whisky into an old-fashioned glass.

2.
Add the ginger wine.

3.
Add a few ice cubes and lightly stir.

4.
Serve immediately.

INGREDIENTS

1¾ ounces Scotch whisky

¾ ounce ginger wine

DAIQUIRI

SERVES 1

INGREDIENTS

1¾ ounces white rum

1 teaspoon lime juice

½ teaspoon sugar syrup

lime wedge, to garnish

1.
Put cracked ice into a cocktail shaker.

2.
Pour the rum, lime juice, and sugar syrup over the ice cubes.

3.
Shake vigorously until well frosted.

4.
Strain into a chilled martini glass and garnish with a wedge of lime. Serve immediately.

Shaking & Stirring

COSMOPOLITAN

SERVES 1

1.
Put cracked ice into a cocktail shaker.

2.
Pour the liquid ingredients over the ice.

3.
Shake vigorously until well frosted.

4.
Strain into a chilled martini glass and garnish with the orange peel. Serve immediately.

INGREDIENTS

1¾ ounces vodka

¾ ounce triple sec

¾ ounce lime juice

¾ ounce cranberry juice

orange peel strip, to garnish

VIRGIN COLLINS

SERVES 1

INGREDIENTS

6 fresh mint leaves, plus extra
to garnish

1 teaspoon superfine sugar

1¾ ounces lemon juice

sparkling water

lemon slice, to garnish

1.
Put the mint leaves into a chilled Collins
or highball glass.

2.
Add the sugar and lemon juice.

3.
Crush the mint leaves, then stir until the
sugar has dissolved.

4.
Fill the glass with cracked ice and top
up with sparkling water. Stir gently and
garnish with the fresh mint and lemon
slice. Serve immediately.

Shaking & Stirring

EL DIABLO

1.
Add the tequila, lime juice, and cassis to a cocktail shaker filled with cracked ice.

2.
Shake vigorously until well frosted. Strain into a chilled highball glass filled with cracked ice.

3.
Top up with ginger ale. Garnish the glass with the lime slice. Serve immediately.

INGREDIENTS

¾ ounce tequila

½ ounce lime juice

½ ounce crème de cassis

ginger ale

lime slice, to garnish

SIDECAR

SERVES 1

1.
Put cracked ice cubes into a cocktail shaker. Pour the liquid ingredients over the ice.

2.
Shake vigorously until well frosted.

3.
Strain into a chilled martini glass and garnish with the orange peel. Serve immediately.

INGREDIENTS

1¾ ounces brandy

¾ ounce triple sec

¾ ounce lemon juice

orange peel, to garnish

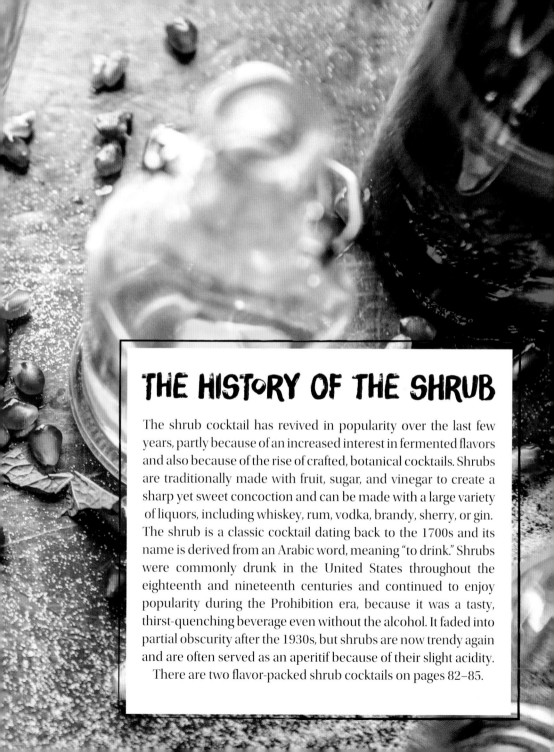

THE HISTORY OF THE SHRUB

The shrub cocktail has revived in popularity over the last few years, partly because of an increased interest in fermented flavors and also because of the rise of crafted, botanical cocktails. Shrubs are traditionally made with fruit, sugar, and vinegar to create a sharp yet sweet concoction and can be made with a large variety of liquors, including whiskey, rum, vodka, brandy, sherry, or gin. The shrub is a classic cocktail dating back to the 1700s and its name is derived from an Arabic word, meaning "to drink." Shrubs were commonly drunk in the United States throughout the eighteenth and nineteenth centuries and continued to enjoy popularity during the Prohibition era, because it was a tasty, thirst-quenching beverage even without the alcohol. It faded into partial obscurity after the 1930s, but shrubs are now trendy again and are often served as an aperitif because of their slight acidity.

There are two flavor-packed shrub cocktails on pages 82–85.

GOOSEBERRY SHRUB

SERVES 1

INGREDIENTS

1⅓ cups fresh gooseberries or ¾ cup canned gooseberries

2 cups superfine sugar

2 cups raw apple cider vinegar

1¾ ounces bourbon

1 teaspoon Angostura bitters

orange wedge, to garnish

FACT
Gooseberries in the US are round and become pink to wine red when they mature—at ½ inch they are smaller than European gooseberries, which can grow to 1 inch in length.

1.
This cocktail takes two days to infuse. In a mixing bowl, muddle the gooseberries and sugar until the gooseberries have broken down. Cover and put into the refrigerator to macerate for 24 hours. Remove from the refrigerator and mix in the vinegar. Cover and return to the refrigerator for another 24 hours.

2.
Strain the liquid through cheesecloth, discarding the solids. Pour the liquid into a sterilized, sealable jar.

3.
Pour 1¾ ounces of the gooseberry syrup into an ice cube-filled old-fashioned glass. Add the bourbon and bitters and stir. Any remaining syrup can be stored in the refrigerator for up to two months. Garnish with the orange wedge and serve immediately.

POMEGRANATE & MINT SHRUB

SERVES 1

INGREDIENTS

1¼ cups pomegranate seeds

2 cups superfine sugar

20 mint leaves

2 cups raw apple cider vinegar

¾ ounce gin

¾ ounce Grand Marnier

sprig of mint, to garnish

1 teaspoon pomegranate seeds,
to garnish

TIP
Try making variations with
other fruits, such as raspberries,
blackberries, strawberries, and
blueberries.

1.
This cocktail takes two days to infuse.
In a bowl, muddle the pomegranate
seeds, sugar, and mint until the seeds
are crushed. Cover and let stand in the
refrigerator to macerate for 24 hours.
Remove from the refrigerator and stir in
the vinegar. Cover again and let stand
for another 24 hours.

2.
Strain the mixture through cheesecloth.
Pour into a sterilized, sealable jar.

3.
Fill a highball glass with crushed ice.
Add 1¾ ounces of the pomegranate
syrup to the glass. The rest of the
pomegranate syrup can be stored in
the refrigerator for up to two months.

4.
Add the gin and Grand Marnier
to the glass and stir with a bar
spoon. Garnish with the mint and
pomegranate and serve immediately.

CRANBERRY COLLINS

SERVES 1

1.
Put cracked ice into a cocktail shaker.

2.
Pour the vodka, elderflower syrup, and cranberry juice over the ice and shake until well frosted.

3.
Strain into a Collins or highball glass filled with cracked ice. Top up with club soda and garnish with the lime slice and peel. Serve immediately.

INGREDIENTS

1¾ ounces vodka

¾ ounce elderflower syrup (cordial)

2½ ounces cranberry juice

club soda

lime slice and lime peel twist,
to garnish

KLONDIKE COOLER

SERVES 1

1.
Put the sugar into a chilled old-fashioned glass and add the ginger ale. Stir until all the sugar has dissolved.

2.
Fill the glass with cracked ice. Pour the whiskey over the ice.

3.
Top up with the sparkling water. Stir gently and garnish with the lemon peel twist. Serve immediately.

INGREDIENTS

½ teaspoon confectioners' sugar

¾ ounce ginger ale

1¾ ounces blended whiskey

sparkling water

lemon peel twist, to garnish

Shaking & Stirring

KIMCHI & WASABI BLOODY MARY

SERVES 1

INGREDIENTS

¾ ounce vodka

¾ ounce sake

½ ounce lime juice

½ teaspoon Korean chili powder

¼ teaspoon garlic granules

1-inch piece fresh ginger, grated

1 teaspoon Thai fish sauce

½ teaspoon wasabi paste

2 teaspoon tonkatsu bulldog sauce or other hot sauce

6 ounces tomato juice

daikon radish stick, to garnish

1.
Mix together the vodka, sake, lime juice, chili powder, garlic granules, ginger, fish sauce, wasabi paste, and bulldog sauce in a Collins or highball glass, using a bar spoon.

2.
Stir well, making sure all the ingredients are well combined.

3.
Add a few ice cubes and the tomato juice and stir again.

4.
Garnish with the daikon radish and serve immediately.

TIP
This drink works well with oysters and you can adjust the seasonings to taste.

BUILDING & LAYERING

BUILDING & LAYERING

Building is a mixology technique and is a technical term for the simple task of pouring all the ingredients, one by one, usually over ice, into the glass in which the cocktail will be served. You might then stir the cocktail briefly, but this is just to mix instead of for chilling or aerating. It is important to follow built recipes exactly, because the order of the ingredients can change from drink to drink and this can affect the final flavor.

Another important skill that the bartender must acquire is the art of layering, which requires greater concentration and precision, and a steadier hand. To make layered shooters or other drinks, you generally first pour the heaviest liquid, working through to the lightest. However, the real trick is the technique. Either touch the top of the drink with a long-handle bar spoon and pour the liquid slowly over the back of it to disperse it across the top of the ingredients already in the glass, or pour the liquid down the twisted stem that many bar spoons have. You should hold the spoon's flat disk just above the drink. Be sure to use a clean bar spoon for each layer. Floating is the term used to describe adding the top layer.

Building & Layering

VODKA ESPRESSO

SERVES 1

INGREDIENTS

1¾ ounces cooled espresso, plus beans to garnish (optional)

¾ ounce vodka

2 teaspoons superfine sugar

¾ ounce Amarula

1.
Put cracked ice into a cocktail shaker.

2.
Pour in the coffee and vodka, add the sugar, and shake vigorously until well frosted.

3.
Strain into a chilled martini glass.

4.
Float the liqueur on top by pouring the Amarula over the back of a teaspoon or bar spoon over the top of the coffee mixture in the glass.

5.
Garnish with coffee beans, if using, and serve immediately.

ELDERFLOWER CHAMPAGNE FIZZ

SERVES 1

INGREDIENTS

7½ cups superfine sugar

4¼ cups water

1 lemon, sliced

15 elderflower heads, washed

2½ tablespoons citric acid (available in supermarkets and health food stores)

½ ounce vodka

5 ounces chilled Champagne

1.
This cocktail takes 24 hours to infuse. In a medium saucepan, bring the sugar and water to a gentle simmer. Turn off the heat and add the lemon slices, elderflower heads, and citric acid. Cover the pan and let infuse for 24 hours.

2.
Strain the syrup through a strainer. Then strain again through cheesecloth to catch all the small parts.

3.
Pour into sterilized, sealable jars. This will keep for several months in a cool place.

4.
Pour ½ ounce of the elderflower syrup into a champagne flute. Add the vodka and then top up with the Champagne.

5.
Serve immediately.

VIRGIN GINGER FIZZ

SERVES 1

1.
Put 1¾ ounces of ginger ale into a blender.

2.
Add the mint sprigs and blend together.

3.
Strain into a chilled highball glass that is filled two-thirds of the way with cracked ice. Top up with more ginger ale.

4.
Garnish with raspberries and the mint sprig. Serve immediately.

INGREDIENTS

ginger ale

3 fresh mint sprigs

fresh raspberries and
a sprig of mint, to garnish

LAYERED ESPRESSO SHOT

SERVES 1

1.
Pour the Galliano into a shot glass.

2.
With a steady hand, to make a second layer, carefully pour in the espresso over the back of a teaspoon or bar spoon that is held against the inside of the glass.

3.
Carefully pour in the heavy cream in the same way to create a third top layer.

4.
Serve immediately.

INGREDIENTS

¾ ounce Galliano

¾ ounce hot espresso

½ ounce heavy cream

AURORA BOREALIS

SERVES 1

1.
Pour the grappa slowly over the back of a spoon down one side of a well-chilled shot glass.

2.
Gently pour the Chartreuse down the other side.

3.
Pour the curaçao gently into the middle.

4.
Add the drops of crème de cassis. Serve immediately.

INGREDIENTS

¾ ounce chilled grappa or vodka

¾ ounce chilled green Chartreuse

½ ounce chilled orange curaçao

3 drops chilled crème de cassis

BELLINI

SERVES 1

1.
Rub the rim of a chilled champagne flute with the lemon wedge.

2.
Put the sugar into a saucer, then dip the rim of the flute in it.

3.
Pour the peach juice into the flute.

4.
Top up with the Champagne.
Serve immediately.

INGREDIENTS

1 lemon wedge

superfine sugar

¾ ounce peach juice

2½ ounces chilled Champagne

NEGRONI

SERVES 1

1.
Put cracked ice into a mixing glass.

2.
Pour the gin, Campari, and vermouth over the ice.

3.
Strain into an old-fashioned glass and garnish with the orange twist. Serve immediately.

INGREDIENTS

¾ ounce gin

¾ ounce Campari

½ ounce sweet vermouth

twist of orange peel,
to garnish

HOT BUTTERED RUM

SERVES 1

INGREDIENTS

¾ ounce dark rum

1 teaspoon packed dark brown sugar

5 ounces hot water

1 teaspoon salted butter

¼ teaspoon allspice

1.
In an old-fashioned glass, mix together the rum, brown sugar, and hot water with a teaspoon until the sugar has completely dissolved.

2.
Place the butter on top.

3.
Sprinkle with the allspice.

4.
When the butter has melted, serve immediately.

WHISKEY SANGAREE

SERVES 1

INGREDIENTS

1¾ ounces bourbon

1 teaspoon sugar syrup

club soda

1 tablespoon ruby port

¼ teaspoon grated nutmeg,
to garnish

1.
Put some ice cubes into a chilled old-fashioned glass.

2.
Pour the bourbon and sugar syrup over the ice.

3.
Top up with club soda.

4.
Stir gently to mix, then pour the port over the top. Sprinkle with the grated nutmeg. Serve immediately.

B-52

1.
Pour the crème de cacao into a shot glass.

2.
With a steady hand, gently pour in the Irish cream over the back of a teaspoon or bar spoon to make a second layer.

3.
Gently pour in the Grand Marnier over the back of a teaspoon or bar spoon.

4.
Serve with layers intact or cover with your hand and slam to mix. Serve immediately.

INGREDIENTS

¾ ounce chilled dark crème de cacao

¾ ounce chilled Irish cream whiskey

¾ ounce chilled Grand Marnier liqueur

A SLOE KISS

1.
Put cracked ice into a cocktail shaker. Pour the sloe gin, Southern Comfort, vodka, and amaretto over the ice and shake vigorously until well frosted.

2.
Strain into a long, chilled highball glass filled with cracked ice.

3.
Splash on the Galliano.

4.
Top up with orange juice and garnish with the orange peel. Serve immediately.

INGREDIENTS

½ ounce sloe gin

½ ounce Southern Comfort

¾ ounce vodka

1 teaspoon amaretto

1 teaspoon Galliano liqueur

orange juice

orange peel twist, to garnish

Building & Layering

KIR ROYALE

SERVES 1

1.
Put the cassis into the bottom of a champagne flute.

2.
Add the brandy.

3.
Top up with Champagne.

4.
Garnish with the mint sprig. Serve immediately.

INGREDIENTS

3 drops crème de cassis, or to taste

½ ounce brandy

Champagne, chilled

fresh mint sprig, to garnish

MOLECULAR COCKTAILS

Molecular mixology originates from the world of experimental gastronomy, where chefs first used molecular techniques in their food recipes. This trend soon caught on and mixologists started using these same methods in their bartending techniques. Molecular mixology is where science combines with cocktails to create some incredible results—from dry ice effects to drinks with overflowing bubbles or frozen nitro cocktails. Other popular molecular techniques include drinks topped with cotton candy, cocktails that have ingredients suspended in the drink, hot infused drinks, cocktails that change color, and cocktail gelatins, ice pops, or marshmallows.

A lot of molecular cocktails created in bars are made with expensive and elaborate equipment, but some of the more simple techniques can be done in the home. Foams and airs can be made in any kitchen, using some basic equipment, and they add an attractive finish to most cocktails (see page 13 for some basic foam and air recipes and page 108 for a foam-topped cocktail). Dry ice can used to produce a dramatic effect and creates an impressive entrance when serving a tray of drinks to friends—a punch served with dry ice can be found on page 110.

MESCAL & WATERMELON FOAM

SERVES 2

INGREDIENTS

1 egg white

½ ounce lemon juice

1 teaspoon superfine sugar

1¾ ounces mescal

¾ ounce triple sec

1¾ ounces watermelon juice

TIP

Foams work well with any fruit-base or sour cocktails.

1.
To make the foam, you need an whip cream dispenser. In a bowl, lightly whisk the egg white, lemon juice, and sugar until the sugar has dissolved. Pour into an whip cream dispenser and charge once.

2.
Put the mescal, triple sec, and watermelon juice into an ice cube-filled cocktail shaker. Shake vigorously until well frosted. Strain the cocktail into two coupe or coupette glasses.

3.
Shake the whip cream dispenser and then top the cocktails with the egg white foam.

4.
Serve immediately.

DRY-ICE PUNCH

SERVES 8

INGREDIENTS

5 ounces bourbon, chilled

5 ounces limoncello, chilled

5 ounces amaretto, chilled

1¾ ounces grenadine

2 cups apple cider, chilled

2 cups orange juice, chilled

2 oranges, sliced

2 apples, sliced

3½ ounces dry ice pellets (optional)

WARNING

Dry ice is a hazardous substance and can cause severe burns if it comes into contact with skin and eyes. Do not leave dry ice unattended around children. Ensure protective gloves, such as oven mitts, are worn at all times when handling the ice, as well as any tools or containers in contact with it. Do not store dry ice in an airtight container and always use in a well-ventilated area. Always read the instructions supplied with dry ice.

1.
Arrange to have the dry ice delivered on the day of use, because it has a short shelf life. You will also need oven mitts and a scoop.

2.
Pour the bourbon, limoncello, amaretto, grenadine, apple cider, and orange juice into a large punch bowl. Add the orange and apple slices.

3.
Place the punch bowl in a large, deep tray filled with water.

4.
If creating the dry ice, use oven mitts and a scoop to transfer the pellets evenly into the water. Serve the punch immediately. The foggy effect will last for only about 5 minutes. Once it has cleared, simply add some more dry ice in the same way.

Building & Layering

TRICOLOR

INGREDIENTS

¾ ounce chilled red maraschino liqueur

¾ ounce chilled crème de menthe

¾ ounce chilled Irish cream

fresh mint leaf, to garnish

1.
Pour the maraschino into a chilled shot glass.

2.
Gently pour in the crème de menthe over the back of a teaspoon or bar spoon to make a second layer.

3.
Gently pour in the Irish cream over the back of a teaspoon or bar spoon.

4.
Garnish with the mint leaf and serve immediately.

RATTLESNAKE

SERVES 1

INGREDIENTS

¾ ounce chilled dark crème de cacao

¾ ounce chilled Irish cream

¾ ounce chilled Kahlúa

cocktail cherry, to garnish

1.
Pour the crème de cacao into a shot glass.

2.
With a steady hand, gently pour in the Irish cream over the back of a teaspoon or bar spoon to make a second layer.

3.
Pour in the Kahlúa over the back of a teaspoon or bar spoon to make a third layer.

4.
Garnish with the cherry and serve immediately.

Building & Layering

AMARETTO, IRISH CREAM & BOURBON

SERVES 1

1.
Gently pour the amaretto into a shot glass.

2.
With a steady hand, carefully pour in the Irish cream over the back of a teaspoon or bar spoon to make a second layer.

3.
Carefully pour in the bourbon in the same way to create a third top layer.

4.
Serve immediately.

┌─ **INGREDIENTS** ─────────

½ ounce amaretto

½ ounce Irish cream

½ ounce bourbon

THE BENTLEY

SERVES 1

1.
Mix the cognac, peach brandy, and passion fruit juice gently together in a chilled mixing glass.

2.
Pour the mixture into a coupe or coupette glass. Add one ice cube and slowly pour in the Champagne.

3.
Serve immediately.

INGREDIENTS

½ ounce cognac or brandy

½ ounce peach brandy or peach schnapps

juice of 1 passion fruit, strained

chilled Champagne

CIDER BREEZE

SERVES 1

1.
Add the rum to a chilled highball glass that is filled halfway with ice cubes.

2.
Top up with the hard cider.

3.
Garnish the glass with the apple slice and serve immediately.

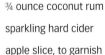 **INGREDIENTS**

¾ ounce coconut rum

sparkling hard cider

apple slice, to garnish

PINK HEATHER

SERVES 1

1.
Pour the whisky and the strawberry liqueur into a chilled champagne flute.

2.
Top up the flute with chilled sparkling wine and garnish the rim of the glass with a strawberry.

3.
Serve immediately.

INGREDIENTS

¾ ounce Scotch whisky

¾ ounce strawberry liqueur

chilled sparkling wine

fresh strawberry, to garnish

Building & Layering

SAZERAC

SERVES 1

INGREDIENTS

1 teaspoon absinthe

½ ounce sugar syrup

¼ ounce Angostura bitters

¼ ounce Peychaud's aromatic bitters

1¾ ounces rye whiskey

lemon zest, to garnish

FACT
The Sazerac is now made with rye whiskey, following the destruction of European vineyards in the nineteenth century, which created a shortage of the Sazarac cognac that gave the cocktail its name.

1.
Swill the absinthe around the inside of an old-fashioned glass.

2.
Add one large ice cube, then the sugar syrup and then both of the bitters and the rye whiskey.

3.
Rub the lemon zest around the rim of the glass.

4.
Serve immediately, with the lemon zest in the glass.

MUDDLING & BLENDING

MUDDLING & BLENDING

Muddling is the term used to describe the extraction of the juice or oils from the pulp or skin of a fruit, herb, or spice. It involves mashing ingredients to release their flavors and it's usually done with a wooden pestlelike implement called a muddler. The end that is used to crush ingredients is thicker and rounded and the opposite, thinner end is used to stir. The best muddling technique is to keep pressing down with a twisting action until the ingredient has released all of its oil or juice. If you don't have a muddler, you can use a mortar and pestle or the end of a wooden spoon. The most well-known muddled drinks are the Mojito and the Caipirinha.

As the name suggests, blending is when all the ingredients are combined together in a blender or food processor. This technique is often used when mixing alcohol with fruit or with creamy ingredients that do not combine well unless they are blended. These drinks are often blended with crushed or cracked ice to produce cocktails with a smooth, frozen consistency. Popular blended drinks are Frozen Daiquiris and Coladas.

LIME & LEMONGRASS SLING

SERVES 1

INGREDIENTS

½ lime

1 small lemongrass stick, trimmed

1¾ ounces gin

½ ounce Benedictine liqueur

½ ounce cherry brandy liqueur

2 dashes orange bitters

5 ounces club soda

lemon slice and fresh cherry,
to garnish

TIP

This recipe is slightly on the dry side
of a traditional sling. If you have a
slightly sweeter tooth, substitute the
club soda with pineapple juice.

1.
Cut the lime into wedges, then slice
the lemongrass thinly.

2.
Put the lime and lemongrass into
a cocktail shaker.

3.
Using a muddler, crush the lime
and lemongrass to release the
juice and oils.

4.
Add the gin, Benedictine, cherry
brandy, and orange bitters to the
cocktail shaker.

5.
Pour the mixture into a sling or
highball glass. Add some ice cubes
and top up with club soda. Garnish
with the lemon slice and cherry and
serve immediately.

BEER & RUM FLIP

SERVES 4

INGREDIENTS

1¼ cups stout

1¾ ounces dark rum

1¾ ounces maple syrup

2 eggs

½ teaspoon nutmeg, to garnish

TIP

This is a great drink for a winter's night or one to celebrate St. Patrick's Day with a bang.

1.
Gently heat the stout in a medium saucepan over medium heat.

2.
Pour the rum and maple syrup into a blender. Crack in the eggs.

3.
When the stout has almost come to a boil, pour it carefully into the blender and blend for 30 seconds, or until the contents are nice and frothy.

4.
Divide the flip between four snifter glasses and garnish each drink with a little nutmeg.

5.
Serve immediately.

Muddling & Blending

RUM COOLER

SERVES 1

1.
Put cracked ice, the rum, pineapple juice, and banana into a blender.

2.
Add the lime juice and blend for about 1 minute or until smooth.

3.
Fill a chilled old-fashioned glass with cracked ice, then pour the cocktail over the ice.

4.
Garnish with the lime peel. Serve immediately.

INGREDIENTS

1½ ounces white rum

1½ ounces pineapple juice

1 banana, peeled and sliced

juice of 1 lime

lime peel twist, to garnish

WHITE RUSSIAN BLENDED SHAKE

SERVES 4

1.
Put all of the ingredients into a blender with a handful of ice cubes and blend thoroughly until smooth.

2.
Divide among four old-fashioned glasses.

3.
Sprinkle each glass with some of the salt.

4.
Serve immediately with a straw.

INGREDIENTS

3½ ounces vodka

3½ ounces Kahlúa

4 scoops vanilla ice cream

½ teaspoon sea salt crystals

Muddling & Blending

MOJITO

1.
Put the sugar syrup, mint leaves, and lime juice into an old-fashioned glass.

2.
Muddle the mint leaves, then add some cracked ice and the rum.

3.
Top up with club soda.

4.
Finish with the Angostura bitters and garnish with the remaining mint leaves. Serve immediately.

INGREDIENTS

1 teaspoon sugar syrup

6 fresh mint leaves, plus extra to garnish

juice of ½ lime

1¾ ounces Jamaican rum

club soda

1 teaspoon Angostura bitters

CAIPIRINHA

SERVES 1

1.
Put the lime wedges into a chilled old-fashioned glass.

2.
Add the sugar to the old-fashioned glass.

3.
Muddle the lime wedges, then pour the cachaça into the glass.

4.
Fill the glass with cracked ice and stir well. Serve immediately.

INGREDIENTS

6 lime wedges

2 teaspoons granulated sugar

2½ ounces cachaça

PIÑA COLADA

SERVES 1

1.
Put the crushed ice into a blender. Pour the white rum, dark rum, and pineapple juice over the ice.

2.
Add the cream of coconut to the blender and blend until smooth.

3.
Pour, without straining, into a chilled goblet or wine glass.

4.
Garnish with the cocktail cherry and the pineapple wedge. Serve immediately.

INGREDIENTS

crushed ice (from 4–6 ice cubes)

1¾ ounces white rum

¾ ounce dark rum

2½ ounces pineapple juice

1¾ ounces cream of coconut

cocktail cherry and pineapple wedge, to garnish

MANDARIN & LIME GINGER BEER

SERVES 1

INGREDIENTS

1 lime

½ mandarin

1¾ ounces dark rum

5 ounces ginger beer

lime wedges, to garnish

1.
Cut the lime and mandarin into wedges.

2.
Put the lime and mandarin into a cocktail shaker. Use a muddler for about 10 seconds to crush the fruit and release its oils.

3.
Add the rum and stir with a bar spoon.

4.
Pour the rum mixture into a Collins or highball glass.

5.
Add a few ice cubes and top up with the ginger beer.

6.
Garnish with lime wedges and serve immediately with a straw.

MIDNIGHT COWBOY

SERVES 1

1.
Slowly blend together the brandy, coffee liqueur, cream, and crushed ice in a blender until frothy.

2.
Pour into a chilled martini glass. Top up with cola and serve immediately.

INGREDIENTS

¾ ounce brandy

½ ounce coffee liqueur

½ ounce light cream, chilled

handful of crushed ice

cola

DIRTY MONKEY HARD SHAKE

SERVES 1

1.
Place the vodka, chocolate syrup, banana, coconut milk, and ice cubes into a blender or food processor.

2.
Blend the mixture for about 1 minute, or until completely smooth.

3.
Pour into a chilled Collins or highball glass.

4.
Garnish with the grated chocolate and serve immediately.

INGREDIENTS

1¾ ounces vodka

1¾ ounces chocolate syrup

1 banana, peeled and chopped

1¾ ounces coconut milk

handful of whole ice cubes

1 teaspoon grated semisweet chocolate, to garnish

BELLE COLLINS

SERVES 1

1.
Muddle the mint sprigs in a mixing glass.

2.
Place the mint in a chilled old-fashioned glass and pour in the gin, lemon juice, and sugar syrup.

3.
Add crushed ice to the glass.

4.
Top up with sparkling water, stir gently, and garnish with more fresh mint. Serve immediately.

INGREDIENTS

2 fresh mint sprigs, plus extra to garnish

1¾ ounces gin

¾ ounce lemon juice

1 teaspoon sugar syrup

sparkling water

Muddling & Blending

MINT JULEP

SERVES 1

1.
Strip the leaves from the mint sprig and put into a chilled old-fashioned glass.

2.
Crush the mint leaves and pour in the sugar syrup.

3.
Fill the glass halfway with cracked ice and stir.

4.
Add the bourbon and garnish with a mint sprig. Serve immediately.

INGREDIENTS

1 fresh mint sprig, plus extra to garnish

1 tablespoon sugar syrup

2½ ounces bourbon

Muddling & Blending

CRAFT INGREDIENTS

Craft cocktails have introduced a whole new range of ingredients into the world of mixology and cocktail menus now feature a huge array of interesting and unusual flavors. Fresh herbs are frequently used in contemporary cocktail making, particularly strong flavors, such as basil, rosemary, thyme, and mint. Other more unusual fresh ingredients include lavender, elderflower, and rose petals, which each add a floral and slightly sweet taste to drinks. Other sweeteners that are used in craft cocktails as alternatives to processed sugars are honey, agave syrup, and maple syrup, which provide a more natural sweetness.

Artisan mixologists also like to infuse other types of drinks into cocktails to create some interesting cocktail hybrids. Tea flavors are popular to use in craft cocktails, from everyday black tea to special blends, such as Earl Grey, green tea, and smoky lapsang souchong. Beer cocktails are becoming more common, using craft ale or stouts mixed with liquors and other ingredients to create strong but flavorful combinations. Hard cider cocktails are also rising in popularity due to the resurgence of craft hard ciders.

PEACH ICE TEA

SERVES 4

INGREDIENTS

2 overripe peaches

¾ ounce tequila

¾ ounce gin

¾ ounce Bacardi rum

¾ ounce triple sec

¾ ounce vodka

¾ ounce lemon juice

¾ ounce lime juice

¾ ounce sugar syrup

2 large handfuls of crushed ice

2¾ cups cola

fresh peach slices, to garnish

TIP
You can also use other soft stone fruits instead of peaches, such as apricots, cherries, or plums, or even pineapple.

1.
Cut the peaches in half, remove the pits, and peel away the skin.

2.
Put all the ingredients, except the cola, into a blender and blend until you have a slushie consistency.

3.
Divide the mixture among four sling or hurricane glasses.

4.
Top up with cola and garnish the glasses with fresh peach slices.

5.
Serve immediately.

BLOODHOUND

SERVES 1

1.
Put the gin, sweet vermouth, dry vermouth, and three strawberries into a blender.

2.
Add the cracked ice.

3.
Blend until smooth.

4.
Pour into a chilled martini glass and garnish with the remaining strawberry. Serve immediately.

INGREDIENTS

1¾ ounces gin

¾ ounce sweet vermouth

¾ ounce dry vermouth

4 strawberries, hulled

cracked ice (from 4–6 ice cubes)

FROZEN PEACH DAIQUIRI

SERVES 1

1.
Put the crushed ice and peach into a blender.

2.
Add the rum, lime juice, and sugar syrup and blend to a slushie consistency.

3.
Pour into a chilled martini glass.

4.
Garnish with the peach slice and serve immediately.

INGREDIENTS

crushed ice (from 4–6 ice cubes)

½ peach, pitted and chopped

1¾ ounces white rum

¾ ounce lime juice

1 teaspoon sugar syrup

peach slice, to garnish

Muddling & Blending

VIRGIN RASPBERRY COOLERS

SERVES 4

1.
Cut the ends off the lemons, then scoop out and chop the flesh.

2.
Put the lemon flesh into a blender with the sugar, raspberries, vanilla extract, and cracked ice and blend for 2–3 minutes.

3.
Fill four highball glasses halfway with cracked ice and strain in the lemon mixture.

4.
Top up with sparkling water and garnish with the mint sprigs. Serve immediately.

INGREDIENTS

2 lemons

1 cup confectioners' sugar

1 cup raspberries

4 drops vanilla extract

cracked ice (from 4–6 ice cubes)

sparkling water

fresh mint sprigs, to garnish

STRAWBERRY COLADA

SERVES 1

1.
Put the crushed ice into a blender.

2.
Add the rum, pineapple juice, and cream of coconut.

3.
Add the strawberries to the blender. Blend until smooth.

4.
Pour, without straining, into a chilled highball glass. Garnish with the pineapple wedge and strawberry half. Serve immediately.

INGREDIENTS

crushed ice (from 4–6 ice cubes)

2½ ounces golden rum

3½ ounces pineapple juice

¾ ounce cream of coconut

6 strawberries

pineapple wedge and halved strawberry, to garnish

Muddling & Blending

FLIRTINI

1.
Put the pineapple into a mixing glass or pitcher.

2.
Crush the pineapple and add the orange liqueur, vodka, and pineapple juice. Stir well.

3.
Strain into a wine or old-fashioned glass.

4.
Top up with the Champagne and serve immediately.

INGREDIENTS

¼ slice fresh pineapple, chopped

½ ounce chilled orange liqueur

½ ounce chilled vodka

¾ ounce chilled pineapple juice

Champagne, chilled

PEACEMAKER PUNCH

SERVES 4

1.
Put the fruit and sugar into a large punch bowl.

2.
Add a little water and crush together, using a muddler.

3.
Add the maraschino and sparkling water and mix well.

4.
Top up with the Champagne. Garnish with the mint leaves and strawberry slices. Serve immediately.

INGREDIENTS

25 strawberries

½ small fresh pineapple, peeled and finely chopped

1–2 tablespoons confectioners' sugar

¾ ounce maraschino liqueur

1 cup sparkling water

1 (750 ml) bottle dry Champagne

fresh mint leaves and sliced strawberries, to garnish

Muddling & Blending

GRAPEFRUIT & CHERRY GIN & TONIC

SERVES 1

INGREDIENTS

1 slice of grapefruit

4 cherries, pitted

1¾ ounces gin

6 ounces tonic water

2 cherries, to garnish

TIP
This would also work with any other citrus fruit, such as oranges, and any other soft fruit, such as blueberries.

1.
Cut the grapefruit slice into chunks.

2.
Place the grapefruit and cherries into a cocktail shaker.

3.
Using a muddler, crush the grapefruit and cherries for about 30 seconds to release the flavor and oils.

4.
Add the gin to the cocktail shaker and stir. Pour the mixture into a Collins or highball glass.

5.
Add some ice cubes to the glass and top up with tonic water.

6.
Garnish with cherries on top and serve immediately.

MOJITO ICE POPS

MAKES 8 ICE POPS

1.
Put the lime juice and club soda into a small bowl and stir together well.

2.
Stir in the mint leaves, lime wedges, sugar, and rum. Using a muddler, mash together all the ingredients until well blended.

3.
Pour the mixture into eight ½-cup ice pop molds. Divide the lime wedges and mint leaves evenly among them. Insert eight ice pop sticks and freeze for 10–12 hours, or until firm.

4.
To unmold the ice pops, dip the frozen molds into warm water for a few seconds and gently release the pops while holding the sticks.

INGREDIENTS

juice of 6 limes

2½ cups chilled club soda

1¼ cups fresh mint leaves

3 limes, cut into wedges

½ cups superfine sugar

1 ounce white rum

BLACK RUSSIAN ICE POPS

MAKES 8 ICE POPS

1.
Put all the ingredients into a small bowl and stir together well.

2.
Pour the mixture into eight ¼-cup ice pop molds or thick shot glasses. Insert eight ice pop sticks and freeze for 8–10 hours, or until firm.

3.
To unmold the ice pops, wrap the frozen molds or glasses in a hot water-soaked dish towel for a few seconds and gently release the pops while holding the sticks.

┌─── **INGREDIENTS** ───────────

½ ounce Kahlúa or Tia Maria liqueur

2 cups cola

1 ounce vodka

└─────────────────────────

BLACKBERRY MARGARITA

SERVES 4

INGREDIENTS

1⅓ cups blackberries

handful of whole ice cubes

1 tablespoon superfine sugar

7 ounces tequila

3½ ounces triple sec

1¾ ounces lime juice

1 lime wedge

1 tablespoon sea salt

4 blackberries, to garnish

4 mint sprigs, to garnish

TIP
This would make a great drink to start or end an evening, because it has a clean, refreshing taste.

1.
Put the blackberries, ice cubes, superfine sugar, tequila, triple sec, and lime juice into a blender.

2.
Blend the mixture for about 1 minute, or until completely smooth.

3.
Rub the rims of four chilled margarita glasses with the lime wedge. Place the sea salt on a small plate and roll the rims in the salt.

4.
Divide the cocktail carefully among the four glasses.

5.
Garnish with the blackberries and mint and serve immediately.

BITTERS & SOURS

BITTERS & SOURS

Using bitters in mixology is a complex process—too much and the drink becomes unpleasant to the taste buds, but the right combination of bitterness with sweetness can produce some tasty, refreshing cocktails. Adding bitters lightly in drops or dashes can help create a slightly addictive taste, and some sweetness or a pinch or two of salt can help reduce the effect of the bitterness. Some common bitters that can be used in mixology are tonic water, bitter lemon, and Angostura bitters, as well as other types of bitters, such as Campari and orange bitters.

Sours were first made in the South in the mid-nineteenth century. They were originally made with brandy before whiskey replaced it as the main liquor of choice, although sours are now often made with gin or vodka, too. Whatever the liquor, the key ingredient of a sour is citrus juice along with a sweetener, such as triple sec, fruit juice, or sugar syrup. Sours are usually mixed by being shaken instead of stirred, and they can sometimes be served in their own special glass, known as a sours glass.

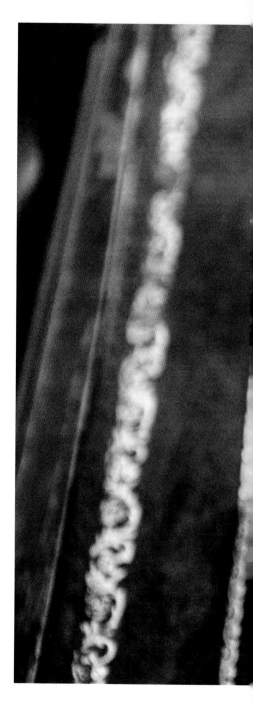

Bitters & Sours

CHAMBORD SOUR

SERVES 1

INGREDIENTS

¾ ounce Chambord

¾ ounce rum

¾ ounce lemon juice

½ egg white

½ ounce sugar syrup

blackberry, to garnish

1.
Chill a coupe or coupette glass.

2.
Put ice cubes into a cocktail shaker. Pour the liquid ingredients over the ice cubes.

3.
Shake the cocktail shaker vigorously until the mixture creates foam.

4.
Strain into the chilled coupe glass.

5.
Garnish the cocktail with the blackberry and serve immediately.

APPLE BRANDY SOUR

SERVES 1

1.
Put ice cubes into a cocktail shaker.

2.
Pour the apple brandy, lemon juice, and sugar syrup over the ice, then shake thoroughly until well frosted.

3.
Fill an old-fashioned glass with ice cubes. Strain the cocktail into the glass.

4.
Garnish the glass with the lemon slice and serve immediately.

INGREDIENTS

1¾ ounces apple brandy

¾ ounce lemon juice

½ ounce sugar syrup

lemon slice, to garnish

CHAMPAGNE BITTERS

SERVES 1

1.
Place the sugar cube in the bottom of a chilled champagne flute.

2.
Add the Angostura bitters.

3.
Pour the brandy over the bitters.

4.
Top up with Champagne and serve immediately.

INGREDIENTS

1 sugar cube

2 teaspoons Angostura bitters

¾ ounce brandy

Champagne, chilled

SOUR APPLE MARTINI

SERVES 1

1.
Put cracked ice into a cocktail shaker.

2.
Pour in the vodka, apple schnapps, and apple juice.

3.
Shake vigorously until well frosted.

4.
Strain into a chilled martini glass and garnish the glass with the apple wedge. Serve immediately.

INGREDIENTS

¾ ounce vodka

¾ ounce sour apple schnapps

¾ ounce apple juice

apple wedge, to garnish

ROB ROY BITTERS

SERVES 1

INGREDIENTS

1¾ ounces Scotch whisky

¾ ounce sweet vermouth

2 teaspoons Angostura bitters

2 teaspoons maraschino syrup, from
the jar

1 piece of lemon zest

maraschino cherry, to garnish

1.
Chill a coupe glass.

2.
Put the Scotch whisky, vermouth, bitters,
and maraschino syrup into an ice cube-
filled cocktail shaker. Stir with a bar spoon.

3.
Twist the lemon zest over the coupe glass
to release its oils and then discard.

4.
Strain the cocktail into the coupe glass.

5.
Garnish the glass with the cherry and
serve immediately.

OLD FASHIONED

SERVES 1

1.
Place the sugar cube into a chilled old-fashioned glass.

2.
Add the Angostura bitters and water. Stir until the sugar has dissolved.

3.
Pour in the bourbon and stir.

4.
Add cracked ice and garnish with the lemon peel. Serve immediately.

INGREDIENTS

1 sugar cube

1 teaspoon Angostura bitters

1 teaspoon water

1¾ ounces bourbon or rye whiskey

lemon peel twist, to garnish

Bitters & Sours

FROZEN RUM SOUR

SERVES 1

1.
Blend the crushed ice in a blender with the light rum, guava juice, lemon juice, and orange juice until it is a slushie consistency.

2.
Pour the frozen mixture into a chilled martini glass.

3.
Serve immediately.

INGREDIENTS

crushed ice (from 4–6 ice cubes)

1¾ ounces light rum

½ ounce guava juice

½ ounce lemon juice

½ ounce orange juice

VIRGIN BITTER GUNNER

SERVES 1

1.
Mix all the ingredients together with some ice cubes in a highball glass.

2.
Taste and add more Angostura bitters, if desired.

3.
Add the lime slice to the glass and serve immediately.

INGREDIENTS

2 ounces lime juice

2 teaspoons Angostura bitters, or to taste

7 ounces ginger beer

7 ounces lemon-flavored soda

lime slice, to garnish

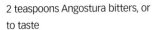

Bitters & Sours

TEQUILA CHERRY COLA

SERVES 1

INGREDIENTS

1¾ ounces tequila

½ ounce triple sec

½ ounce sour cherry syrup

3½ ounces cola

lime wedge, to garnish

TIP

This would be a great drink to enjoy with tacos or nachos at a barbecue.

1.
Pour the tequila into an ice cube-filled old-fashioned glass.

2.
Add the triple sec and sour cherry syrup to the glass.

3.
Top up with the cola.

4.
Garnish with the lime wedge and serve immediately.

CRAFT DECORATION

With really simple cocktails, decoration can be as basic as just adding a single twist of lemon or lime peel to the rim of the glass. But to create some truly beautiful craft cocktails, try experimenting with a range of decoration styles. Botanical cocktails can look great just by adding sprigs of natural herbs in and around the glass, such as thyme sprigs, lemon verbena, mint, lemon balm, or feathery fennel leaves, or try decorating with slices or pieces of the natural fruit used in the recipe, such as pomegranate seeds or berries. For decorating with foams and air, see page 13 and for molecular techniques, see page 107.

Another attractive way to add color and fragrance to cocktails is by using edible flowers or petals. You can use large flowers for a dramatic effect or smaller flowers and petals for a more delicate look or for adding to ice cubes or ice pops. Some popular large edible flowers are coriander flowers, lavender sprigs and flowers, and pansies. Some common small edible flowers are cornflowers, borage, rose petals, elderflowers, and violas. Use home-grown flowers that have not been sprayed with insecticides, or if buying them from a farmer's market or other supplier, ask if they are organic to make sure they are edible.

SHERRY, ARMAGNAC & DRAMBUIE BITTERS

SERVES 1

INGREDIENTS

1¾ ounces armagnac

½ ounce Amontillado sherry

1 teaspoon Angostura bitters

½ ounce Drambuie

orange wedge, to garnish

TIP

This is a classic nightcap or a way
to wind down after a big meal at a
dinner party.

1.
Pour the Armagnac, sherry, bitters,
and Drambuie into an ice cube-filled
old-fashioned glass.

2.
Stir with a bar spoon.

3.
Garnish with the wedge of orange and
serve immediately.

BOURBON SOUR

SERVES 1

1.
Put the lemon juice, bourbon, and sugar into a cocktail shaker filled with ice cubes.

2.
Shake vigorously until well frosted. Strain into a martini glass or sours glass.

3.
Garnish with a slice of orange and serve immediately.

INGREDIENTS

¾ ounce lemon or lime juice

1¾ ounces bourbon

1 teaspoon superfine sugar

orange slice, to garnish

STREGA SOUR

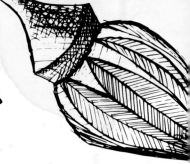

SERVES 1

1.
Put the gin, Strega, and lemon juice into a cocktail shaker filled with ice cubes.

2.
Shake vigorously until well frosted. Strain into a martini glass or sours glass.

3.
Garnish with a slice of lemon and serve immediately.

INGREDIENTS

1¾ ounces gin

¾ ounce Strega liqueur

¾ ounce lemon juice

lemon slice, to garnish

BROKEN NEGRONI

SERVES 1

1.
Add the vermouth and bitters to a mixing glass filled with ice cubes and stir.

2.
Strain into a chilled champagne flute.

3.
Top up with sparkling wine and garnish the glass with the orange slice. Serve immediately.

INGREDIENTS

¾ ounce sweet vermouth

¾ ounce Campari bitters

sparkling wine

half a thin slice of orange, to garnish

WHISKEY SOUR

SERVES 1

1.
Put cracked ice into a cocktail shaker and pour over the whiskey.

2.
Add the lime juice.

3.
Add the sugar and shake well.

4.
Strain into a martini or wine glass and garnish with the slice of lime and a cherry. Serve immediately.

INGREDIENTS

1¾ ounces blended whiskey

¾ ounce lime juice

1 teaspoon confectioners' sugar or sugar syrup

lime slice and cocktail cherry, to garnish

BOSTON SOUR

1.
Place cracked ice into a cocktail shaker.

2.
Pour the lemon juice, whiskey, and sugar syrup over the ice.

3.
Add the egg white. Shake until chilled.

4.
Strain into a martini glass and garnish with the lemon slice and a cocktail cherry. Serve immediately.

INGREDIENTS

¾ ounce lemon juice
or lime juice

1¾ ounces blended whiskey

1 teaspoon sugar syrup

1 egg white

lemon slice and cocktail cherry,
to garnish

BLOOD ON THE TRACKS

SERVES 1

1.
Pour the bitters into a chilled highball glass filled with ice cubes.

2.
Add the juice. Do not stir.

3.
Top up with sparkling water.

4.
Garnish with the orange slice and mint and serve immediately.

INGREDIENTS

½ ounce Campari bitters

2½ ounces blood orange juice

sparkling water

orange slice and fresh mint sprig, to garnish

INDEX

INDEX - BY COCKTAIL

Honey, Peach & Agave
  Infusion 33
Hot Buttered Rum 101
Kimchi & Wasabi Bloody
  Mary 88
Kir Royale 105
Klondike Cooler 87

Layered Espresso Shot 97
Lime & Lemongrass Sling
  124

Mandarin & Lime Ginger
  Beer 133
Manhattan 61
Margarita 63
Martini 65
Matcha Green Tea Vodka
  Refresher 38
Mescal & Watermelon
  Foam 108
Midnight Cowboy
  134
Mint Julep 137
Mojito 130
Mojito Ice Pops 150

Negroni 100

Old Fashioned 163

Peacemaker Punch 147
Peach & Basil Gin Fix 37
Peach Ice Tea 140
Piña Colada 132
Pink Heather 117
Plum & Ginger Whiskey
  Fizz 34
Pomegranate & Mint
  Shrub 84

Rattlesnake 113
Rhubarb & Vanilla Bourbon
  Cocktail 30
Rob Roy Bitters 162
Rosemary Vodka Cooler 44
Rum Cobbler 66
Rum Cooler 128

Sazerac 118
Sherry, Armagnac &
  Drambuie Bitters 170
Sidecar 79
Sour Apple Martini 161
Strawberry Colada 145
Strega Sour 173

Tequila Cherry Cola 166
The Bentley 115
Tom Collins 70
Tricolor 112
Turkish Delight Gin
  Cocktail 58

Virgin Bitter Gunner 165
Virgin Collins 77
Virgin Ginger Fizz 96
Virgin Raspberry Coolers
  144
Vodka Espresso 94

Whiskey Sangaree 102
Whiskey Sling 62
Whiskey Sour 175
White Russian Blended
  Shake 129

INDEX – BY SPIRIT

This edition published by Parragon Books Ltd in 2016 and distributed by

Parragon Inc.
440 Park Avenue South, 13th Floor
New York, NY 10016
www.parragon.com/lovefood

LOVE FOOD is an imprint of Parragon Books Ltd

ISBN 978-1-4748-1748-6

Printed in China

New recipes: Lincoln Jefferson
New and cover photography: Mike Cooper
Designer: Beth Kalynka
Senior Editor: Cheryl Warner

Notes for the Reader

This book uses both metric and imperial measurements. Follow the same units of measurement throughout; do not mix metric and imperial. All spoon measurements are level: teaspoons are assumed to be 5 ml, and tablespoons are assumed to be 15 ml. One measure is assumed to be 25 ml/¾ fl oz. Unless otherwise stated, milk is assumed to be full fat, eggs and individual fruits and vegetables are medium, pepper is freshly ground black pepper and salt is table salt. A pinch of salt is calculated as $\frac{1}{16}$ of a teaspoon. Unless otherwise stated, all root vegetables should be peeled prior to using.

The times given are an approximate guide only. Preparation times differ according to the techniques used by different people and the cooking times may also vary from those given.

Please consume alcohol responsibly.